P9-DFP-207

Restaurant:
The Owner's Manual

A Guide to Staff Training for
Owners and Management

Restaurant:
The Owner's Manual

A Guide to Staff Training for Owners and Management

Larry O. Knight, Master Butler

Copyright © 2011 by Larry O. Knight, Master Butler.

| ISBN: | Softcover | 978-1-4568-6706-5 |
| | Ebook | 978-1-4568-6707-2 |

All rights reserved. No part of this book may be reproduced or transmitted in any form or by any means, electronic or mechanical, including photocopying, recording, or by any information storage and retrieval system, without permission in writing from the copyright owner.

This book was printed in the United States of America.

To order additional copies of this book, contact:
Xlibris Corporation
1-888-795-4274
www.Xlibris.com
Orders@Xlibris.com
94570

CONTENTS

FORWARD

This book is designed to educate, enlighten and energize Owners, Management and Staff.

It is this author's desire to restore a sense of caring, an eye for detail and a raising of standards in the exciting profession of Restaurant service. We cover language, product knowledge and professional standards.

We know you will find this book helpful and when the contents are applied, beneficial to your bottom line. And, after all, isn't that what it is all about?

DEDICATION

To Jimmie, Dan, and all the gang at Gaslamp Quarter Association.
Thanks for your encouragement and your kindness.
Larry O. Knight, Master Butler

CHAPTER 1
For the Server: Getting Started

Go See What it Looks Like

Pick the best restaurant you can afford, and go more than once, if possible. Notice any differences in the service from one visit to the other. Ask questions; take notes.

Is this what you really want to do? Could you do a better job than most of the waiters you've had experience with?

Be critical of all you observe. Ask yourself what you would change and why.

If you're just starting out, ask for help. False pride will get you nowhere. Most people will be happy to give you hints and help if you drop the know-it-all attitude. In fact, I've found that most people, if properly approached, are very flattered by a request for help.

Very few people start out at the top, so be patient. And be on the alert for every opportunity to sharpen your skills. No matter how modest the operation, never work for a place you cannot be proud of, both out front and back of the house.

Knowledge is Power!

You will feel much more comfortable if your manner and knowledge are equal to, if not surpassing, that of those you serve.

Be aware that you can learn a great deal from your guests. It's okay not to know everything, and it's okay to ask the guest to explain to you exactly what he or she wants, if you don't quite understand.

Research

Know all the various pieces of silver, china, glassware, etc. used in table settings. Browse the shelves at your local library for books on table manners and table settings. Visit fine china and silver shops and departments at upscale department stores. Ask for and study any brochures they may offer.

CHAPTER 2
What Every Service Should Know

Silver Setup

Forks at the guest's left; knives and spoons at the right. A note to your knaves on knives: All knife blades should be facing inward, toward the dinner plate, never outward (too threatening). Dessert spoon and fork are placed on the table at the head of the plate, with spoon in the lower position, bowl end facing left; fork is placed above spoon, tines facing right. Got it?

The guest should work the setup from the outside inward but don't count on that happening all the time. Just set up the needed silver and let them have at it.

If your guest sets the knife and fork, tines down, parallel across the plate, with the handles near four o'clock, this is the formal way of signaling they are done. Even so, be sure to ask, "May I clear, Miss Dennis?"

Napkin Folding

Elaborate napkin folds are old-fashioned, unsanitary, and fussy. Management, please take note: Simple folds are easier and faster to do, and are much more elegant than swans, et al. I have spoken.

Tools of the Trade

Carry with you:

1. A very good wine bottle opener
2. A working cigarette lighter and two packs of matches (keep them in a "dry" pocket)
3. Two working pens and a note pad (again, keep in a dry pocket)
4. A crumbler (that little scoop for cleaning off tables after you have cleared, or as needed)
5. A cigar tip cutter (if appropriate to your particular situation)

You and Your Guests

Please keep in mind that your guests are your clients and patrons. Without them, you don't have a job. The guest may be wrong, but it is not your job or obligation to point that out. Conversely, you are not always right. When a mistake is made, it is your job and obligation to promptly correct it to the complete satisfaction of all concerned.

Being a waiter means never having to say, "I'm sorry!" No matter what terrible thing you have done or mistake you have made. A professional waiter always says, "Please forgive me!" and keeps saying it until the guests actually do. (And they will!)

It's all in the Details

Describe everything you put in front of your guests, in detail, to the best of your ability. "The cream of Jerusalem artichoke soup, sir"; "Your crown roast of lamb with scalloped eggplant"; "Our garden-fresh braised baby spinach." Your guests may not listen to you, but you will have done your part.

And know your ingredients! Be ready, willing, and able to describe in detail the ingredients of every dish on the menu.* Your guests *will* ask, so be prepared. Many people suffer from serious allergies, and there are also religious and cultural concerns over certain ingredients. Do you homework.

If something is amiss—the restaurant is short-handed, the air-conditioning has gone awry, etc.-your guests deserve and explanation up front, not after the fact.

Give them a reason, not an excuse. Offer a freebie, if allowed, up front, and let them know you're on their side and will do all you can to keep things moving along. Remenber, "Please forgive us, but . . ." and do it *before* they get angry and hostile!

A Language Lesson

A note to owners, managers, and staff:

- Your first greeting should ALWAYS be "Welcome!"
- Your most important tools are your eyes! Look-see-act.

Amateur vs. Professional

(It Makes All the Difference in the World)
Amateur: Avoid these phrases at all costs.
Professional: Rehearse and use these guest-friendly phrases instead.

Amateur: "No problem!" (Absolutely the worst!)
Professional: "Very good, sir/madam." "Certainly. I'll see to it immediately." Or "You're welcome." (What a concept.)

Amateur: "Yeah."
Professional: "Yes, sir/ Mr./ Mrs. Jones "

Amateur: "Sure," or even worse, "Shurr."
Professional: "Of course, Mr./ Mrs. Blank," or "Very good, sir/ma'am."

Amateur: "Bye now" or "buh-bye"; And "Have a nice day," is about as tired as it gets.
Professional: "Good evening/ good day, Dr. Brown."

Amateur: "you bet!" "Okey-dokey." Etc..
Professional: "Very good, Mrs. Wilson," or "I'll see to it immediately."

Amateur: "Oh NO!" "Not again!" or "Sorry!"

Professional: "Thank you for calling that to my attention, Mr. Jones." (A good phrase to use when something is amiss.)

Amateur: "Is everything okay?"
Professional: "Is everything to your satisfaction?"

Amateur: "How about [some dessert, a cuppa coffee, or something]?"
Professional: "May I offer [dessert, coffee, etc..]?"

Amateur: "Are you through?" "Are you done?" "Are you still working on that?"
Professional: "May I clear?" "May I Remove?"
Please do not reach at the same time. Wait for answer!

And "Take your time" is a definite no-no at any time.

Note: Never offer "or something." Always be specific.
Example: For dessert, we have apple pie, vanilla pudding.

And, of course, a professional would never use profanity of any kind. A guest's foul mouth is not an invitation for you to respond in kind.

Where There's Smoke

If you have a smoker at your table, watch that ashtray. Never let more than two butts accumulate before you remove the ashtray and replace it with a fresh one.

House Policy

What is House Policy? You need to know what you can comp (offer without charge) to make amends for a mistake or an error.

By getting very clear on such company policy, you will appear to be the competent waiter you are.

Always maintain a clear understanding with management as to what you can or cannot do to rectify any unfortunate situation. In the following situations, what is house policy?

Example 1: The guest has eaten all of his entrèe and *then* complains it was awful.

Example2: The guest eats a couple of bites of entrèe and complains right away.

Credit Cards

Know which credit cards your company accepts and which ones they do not. Check all cards for the expiration date. If expired, call this to the guest's attention in a discreet manner.

If card company denies payment: again, discreetly advise the guest and ask for another card for submission.

Know, before the fact, if the company accepts checks, and if so, what kind: i.e., personal, corporate, third party.

---

*Host/hostess/Maitre D must know the menu as well as the servers do, and be aware of daily specials. They should also know the neighborhood, local points of interest, banks, shopping, and transportation.

CHAPTER 3

And We're Off to "Never-Never Land"

Do Not Try This At Work

- NEVER cheat your employer, or your guests, out of what is rightfully theirs: your time and full attention to their needs.

- NEVER touch or lean against a chair, occupied or not, at a table, once the guests are seated. I have seen this rule violated in the very smartest restaurants. Is everyone so tired that they can't stand up straight? The only exception to this rule: Waiter may (and should) help adjust chairs for guests, upon their arrival and their departure ("May I?" or "Allow me").

- Please do not stand with your arm folded behind you, fist in the small of your back. That is okay in Europe, but is a sure sign of an amateur here in the USA. Keep your hands in front of you, or at your sides, after all, you may need to use them quite suddenly.

- Always check your tables as you pass by. Smile at your guests, and glance at the table to see if they may be in need of something, *before* they ask. Care.

- Please do not avoid eye contact when a guest is trying to get your attention, even if you're very busy. Acknowledge each guest and signal that you'll be with them in a moment, or as soon as possible. They will love and appreciate you for that small gesture of kindness.

- It goes without saying your guests should NEVER have to ask for more water, bread, or butter. But, of course, you knew that.

- NEVER touch a guest unless it is an emergency. For example: they are falling over or have stumbled.

- NEVER offer a handshake. If a guest offers his hand, be gracious enough to shake it.

- Avoid chatting with your guests, and NEVER, ever, interject yourself into any conversation going on at the table, as tempting as it sometimes may be. Do not laugh at or acknowledge, in any way, a joke of any kind that may be going on at the table, unless it is very obvious that you are included in the festivities. Save yourself from a very embarrassing situation by following the above rule.

- NEVER offer any personal comments about yourself, your family, or friends. Usually, the guest could care less about your personal affairs. Should a guest ask a personal question, answer as succinctly as possible and move on.

- NEVER say anything, anywhere, to anyone, which is derogatory about any guest, period! Your negativity can and will cost you money. A lot. Get over it, and get on with it.

- NEVER get too chummy with the guests. Familiarity breeds contempt.
  Ex: *Situation*: A guests asks you to call him by his first name.
       Solution: Say, "Please forgive me, Mr. Smith, it is against house rules." (Even if it is not, it should be against your own *personal rule*). Therefore, NEVER call your guests by their first names, even if they insist. As someone once said, "New friends don't tip friends," and it's true. Of course, *real* friends usually take very good care of us!

- NEVER discuss anything personal with other staff while on or near the floor or anywhere your guests could possibly overhear it. NEVER!

Ex: *Situation*: Another staff member wants to chat while you're on
      duty, on the floor.
      Solution: "Let's talk about it on break, okay?"

Odds and Ends to Avoid

Don't fuss with your hair or uniform. Do not scratch an itch while on the
floor. It is very unattractive.

Avoid really ugly shoes. Believe me, people notice these things. Wear plain,
comfortable, black, dress shoes (no sneakers, please).

Leave your expensive rings and watches at home. Nobody tips Mr. or Ms.
"Rich Bitch."

The Paragraph I Would Rather Not Have Had to Write

Do I really have to say anything about bad breath, dirty nails, unpolished
shoes, wrinkled, frayed, or soiled uniforms, or chewing gum while on
duty? If I do, you're in the wrong business. And please, Snow White and
the Seven Dwarfs notwithstanding, no whistling. Thank you.

Don't Rush

Try not to appear frazzled, harried, or rushed, even on the busiest night of
the year. The secret here is to *do one thing at a time and do it right*.

Be economical with your movements. Remember the old "take something
out and bring something back" rule. If you do not mentally get ahead of
yourself, staying instead in the *now*, you'll be all right. If you keep thinking
ahead to all you have to do, chaos will reign supreme.

A Guest's Thanks

It is not appropriate, nor should it be expected, that the guests thank you
every time you fill the water glass, or as you serve dessert, etc. A guest's "thank
you" at the end of the meal, when paying the check, is sufficient if the quality
of your service warrants it. And don't forget to thank *them* for coming: "It's
been a pleasure to serve you. We look forward to seeing you again soon."

CHAPTER 4
Into Action—And Away We Go

Checking In

Before you start the workweek, take a few minutes to copy down your schedule from the bulletin board. This eliminates the possibility of coming in late, which could result in disciplinary action. Be sure to check the starting time for your station. Also check the board for any new information that may have been posted.

You should be dressed and ready to work when your shift begins. Hands must be clean. You must have a pen, crumber, and wine opener before you start your shift. Your uniform must be neat, clean, and pressed. (See *Appearance*)

Opening duties include:

- Making sure the menu covers and pages are clean and neat.
- Making sure the menus contain the correct pages for lunch and dinner.
- Reviewing your reservations for the day and notifying servers of large parties.

Food Servers:

Before you go out to your station, check the kitchen for pertinent notices and specials. If there is no description of how the specials are prepared, ask the chef or manager.

The server is responsible for every aspect of service including the initial approach to the table, greeting the customer, taking the drink order and delivering the same, relating specials, taking food orders, timing of food preparations, timing with regard to sequence of service (so that no Course will ever overlap another and no course will ever be served more than five minutes after the previous course has been cleared), taking dessert and after dinner drink orders, presentation of the check, correct credit card procedures, and making correct change. This also includes the appearance of all food served, cleanliness and orderliness of the table, and, in general, the overall success of service to the customer. Proper coordination and communication with your busser and food runner is essential, since, as a server, you are in charge of giving direction to your busser. It will be helpful for you to be aware of the priorities of his/her responsibilities. Organization is imperative.

Food Runner:

The food runner expedites customer food orders, making sure the are properly prepared, complete, and ready for delivery to all guests at a given table in a timely manner. Make sure the food presentation is correct before leaving the kitchen. Check to make sure that you are delivering the proper order to the proper guest. It is your responsibility to know the location of all table numbers and seat positions.

Busser:

The main function of a busser is to clean and reset tables, and serve bread, water, coffee, and tea. The server will direct the busser with priorities and communicate with them to ensure his/her efficiency. With proper guidance, the busser should help with cleaning plates, keeping the table clean, and providing invaluable aid to other areas of servicing the table.

Busser opening duties include:

- Making coffee and iced tea
  - Iced tea: Check the quality of what is already made and make new if needed. Restock tea bags for brewing. Keep the brewing pot, storage pot, and serving pots clean and full. Inform management if stock is low.*

- o Coffee: Clean the machine regularly as indicated by the manufacturer. Restock filters, coffee, decaf, pots, etc., and keep the area clean and stocked with creamers, and sweeteners. Milk; Half & Half; even Chocolate syrup.*
- Setting up bus carts/tubs on each side of kitchen
- Cutting lemons
- Filling ice bins
  - o Ice: Clean, stocked, and scoops readily available.*
- Stocking bread
  - o Bread Service: Area clean and fully stocked with napkins, plates, baskets, and serving tongs.*
  - o Bread: Fresh and ready.*
  - o Butter: Clean and serving dishes stocked.*
- Folding napkins for bread baskets
- Restocking linen
- Polishing silverware and glassware as needed
  - o Cracker Trays: Refilled and cleaned.*
  - o Salt and Pepper: Refilled and cleaned.*
  - o Sugar Dishes: Refilled and cleaned.*
  - o Napkins: Cloth, paper, and cocktail stocked with backup.*
  - o Computer Paper/Credit Card Paper: Stocked with backup.*
  - o To Go: Restock and organize (boxes/bags/sauce cups).*
  - o Salad: Is it fresh or is it brown? You have the right to refuse service to any ugly salad.*
  - o Salad Extras: Bacon, Onions, Croutons, Tomatoes, etc..*
  - o Dressings: Fresh, clean, correctly labeled.*
  - o Containers: Fresh, clean, full with proper ladles.*

Setting Up Your Station

All servers are expected to know all table numbers and different station delineations. Before setting up your station, know who your busser is and review your expectations with them. Once at your station, check the following:

- Make sure your table and chairs are clean, and that seats are free of stains or crumbs. Chairs should be straight with the table. Clean and dust all the chairs, tops, sides, underneath the seats, and the legs. Check for broken or weak chairs and report to management.*

- If Chairs are needed, take them from around the outside walls rather than from tables that are already set up.
- Make sure ice buckets are clean and ready for use.
- Napkins should be folded neatly, and centered on each place setting.
- Check your silverware to make sure it is properly arranged and that surfaces are absolutely spotless.
- Make sure glassware is polished and properly arranged.
- Make sure sugars, salt, and peppershakers are filled to the top and wiped clean. Sugar caddy should contain sugar, Equal, and Sweet & Low. Caddy should be full but not so packed that it is difficult to get the envelopes out.
- Check the floor in your station to make sure it was swept and that any dried spots or spills have been wiped up. In a word, the floor must be spotless.
  - o Floors: Make sure to check the entrances to the bathrooms. Do not assume that the least paid employee is doing their job better than you do yours. During the workday or night, make a habit of looking down. There is always something down there for you to pick-up!*
  - o Clean all surfaces: Shelves and cabinets. Restock and use proper spray cleaners and towels for the surfaces you clean.*
  - o Laundry: Clean and dirty do not belong together. Both should be maintained from start to end of shift. Do not waste but do not compromise health for thrift.*
  - o Trash: Line the containers and make sure the containers are washed and free of odors. Check regularly for trash levels and empty as needed. Do not put the trash containers near food preparation or service areas or anywhere silverware might fall into them.*

If you have any questions regarding the proper set-up and cleanliness of your stations, ask your manager.

YOU ARE RESPONSIBLE FOR THE OVERALL APPEARANCE OF YOU STATION!

Servers Opening Side Work

AM SHIFT:

1. Check the entire dining room, making sure that everything on the table is very clean and set properly.
2. Steam and buff glasses and silverware as needed.
3. Fold napkins as needed; you should have a supply of 100. A simple fold is best.
4. Stock computer stations with extra paper rolls and ribbon.
5. Wipe clean all cruvinet cards and wine lists.
6. Place flower vases on center of tables.

PM SHIFT:

1. Make sure dining room is properly set and clean, including large party tables reserved early to avoid moving tables during business hours.
2. Make sure that all sugar caddies, salt, and peppershakers are filled and cleaned.
3. Make sure all glasses and silverware are clean, polished, and properly set, stocked, and matching on each table.*
4. Fold enough napkins so that you always have a supply of 100. A simple fold is best.

Take pride in your work! This is an element of care and concern.

Don't just do the minimum; take pride in a job well done!

A word on teamwork: COVER EACH OTHER! If you are getting buried, ASK FOR HELP! Everyone will need help at one time or another, whether it is when serving our guests or doing side work. It all evens out.

Pick things up—Return them to their proper place.

Don't be sloppy, pick up after yourself and each other!!!

Phone Etiquette

Attention Maitre D', Host /Hostess, ET AL.

Don't let the telephone intimidate you. The guest in front of you is all-important and takes priority over any calls coming in after they have presented themselves for seating. If no one is available to cover the phone, let it ring until you return. You wouldn't stop to answer the phone if you were seating the Queen of England, would you?

If you're on the phone when guests arrive, conclude the call as quickly as possible and then attend to your arrivals. Never let a guest experience anything but the most professional demeanor and courtesy as they await your attention. Certainly, guests should never hear a personal conversation, or telephone rudeness of any kind.

Everyone on the floor, from owners and managers on down, should know how to answer the telephone properly.

It's: "Good Evening . . . Piero;s Restaurant. (Pause) This is John. How may I help you?"

If you must transfer the call, ask who is calling, and be careful not to disconnect the customer. If you must take a message, get the customer's full name (ask for correct spelling), repeat the phone number back to the guest to make sure it is right, and ask the nature of the call. There should be a pen and pad at every phone outlet, and all phone messages should be written out and complete. Employees with poor English skills should be advised to not answer the phone.

Greeting Guests—"Welcome!"

When greeting your guests, the all-time, absolute No. 1 customer relations' rule is: *Call your guests by name!* Do it, do it often, and do it right (doctors prefer to be called Dr., and some women prefer Ms. to Mrs.). Nothing will please them more, and guess what happens when your guests are pleased?

Host/Hostess:

The hostess is the first person with whom the customer comes into contact. You must wear professional business attire whenever on duty. Casual attire is not allowed. The hostess offers the first and the last impression of the restaurant, and is in the position to offer the kind of recognition and reassurance that will help make regular customers for the restaurant.

When greeting customers in person, say: "Welcome to Piero's—I am (*your name*), may I help you?" The hostess should try to call customers by name and be able to smooth over any delays in seating or interruption in service. If you do not know the guests name, address them as "Sir" or "Madam."

Servers:

Greet your customers with "Welcome!" This is the first thing you do when customers are seated. Even if you are busy and can't do anything else, acknowledge their presence. Within the first two minutes a party is seated, you must at least stop by and tell them you will be with them shortly. This is a must!!! As you first approach the table, let cheerfulness shine through as you introduce yourself. SMILE! Address guests as "Sir" or "Madam." Notify the manager of any "VIP" guests that you may be serving. Always stand up straight. Do not lean on chairs, tables, or booths.

When You Assume

In a resort area, when taking reservations, make a note if guest is a visitor or local. Use a V (for visitor), including hotel name, and an L (for local) on your reservation sheet, and pass this on to the appropriate parties when guests arrive. Locals will love being acknowledged (so very *in*, don't you know) and visitors will be very impressed that you know their hotel and that they are your guests from out of town. And after all, isn't that what you're being paid for?

And Yet Another Note On Assuming

A couple is not always husband and wife, so it might be Mr. Smith, yet not Mrs. Smith. Be careful in this area and only go with what you know for sure. Assuming any relationship could prove embarrassing.

Seating Guests

Again, maitre d', host/hostess (or anyone seating guests): Take your time. Invite everyone at the table to enjoy their dinner, lunch, or whatever (look 'em in the eye and SMILE) and offer the menus *individually*. The wine list should be offered after the orders are taken. Never just plop menus down and walk off. Treat your guests the way you would like to be treated if you were in the finest restaurant in the world.

One of the primary jobs of the hostess id to seat the restaurant and to do so in an equitable manner. This means that the dining room should be filed by seating each station with approximately the same number of people.

Taking & Serving Orders

When it looks like your party is ready, approach the table and describe the specials in an appetizing manner. Never recommend anything or offer any suggestions regarding any particular dish, unless, of course, management requests you do so. You will just be asking for it—trouble, that is.

If you *are* asked, assure your guests that they will undoubtedly enjoy whatever they select. If pushed into giving your suggestions, rely on that old standby: "I'd rather not recommend anything in particular since we all have different tastes. However, the chef's signature dishes are blah, blah, and blah." Or, "The special of the house is blah, blah, blah."

Once they have made their selections (never use the word "choice"), heartily endorse them after the fact. "An excellent selection, Dr. Green." You may even want to give an affirmative nod, accompanied by a pleased and pleasant smile for all to see.

And NEVER auction off the service, i.e., "who has the steak well done?" Unless you have a perfect memory, avoid this very unprofessional approach by writing down the chairs by number before taking the orders and then filling in the order for each chair. Be creative and be professional. When you input the order in the computer, be sure to have the right table number and the proper guest number, it is essential that every item be entered on the ticket. Kitchen personnel will not process any order unless it has been entered into the computer.

Once you have mastered the skills and the language, and developed the proper attitude, waiting becomes performance. So, sing with your heart, and dance with your every movement. It's show time and every shift becomes opening night!

NOTE: Do not leave your guest unattended. Stay in view of the guests as much as possible. Always check the tables in your station to determine if there is anything you might be able to get your guests. Once again, this is an element of organization.

As part of your training, you must be totally certain of cooking times for ordering any given item from the menu. If an order is not accurately timed you will be wasting valuable minutes that could be spent on the floor. It also bogs down the kitchen for others who are timing their orders to avoid overlapping. This is an important time to mention that management expects no course to overlap. **This is a cardinal sin!** Also, make sure that no course is served more than five minutes after the previous course has been cleared, unless the guest request a delay. Needless to say, poor timing also creates extra work and unnecessarily irritates the kitchen staff, which is cooking under a great deal of pressure.

NOTE ON TIMING: We will repeat it again because it is important. NEVER LET ONE COURSE OVERLAP ANOTHER! In others words, do not serve the salad when the soup is still being consumed, etc.. Always wait until everyone in the party is through with a particular course before serving the next one. For example: do not serve soup until everyone is through with the appetizer (unless otherwise requested by the customer). Never remove a plate until everyone at the table is finished with that particular course. Example: Do not serve entrees until the salad plates and forks have been removed. You may go ahead and remove a plate, however, only if a customer obviously wishes the plate removed by pushing it aside, or he simply asks you to do so.

Approximately two or three minutes after the food is served, check to make sure everyone is enjoying their meal and that nothing else is needed. Correct any problems immediately. If you cannot correct the problem, notify your manager. This is a good time to suggest more cocktails or more wine and to clear away all empty cocktail and wine glasses.

Remove the salt and peppershakers at the end of the meal when you crumb the table. This is a continual effort. Don't wait for the busser to do this. You are responsible for your station. The busser's primary responsibility is to clear and reset the tables after the customers have left and to bring bread and pate' to the tables.

When you can see that the customers are almost ready for their food, call it from the food runner. You are responsible for coordinating your entire order along with the food runner. When serving food and drinks, be careful to keep your finger away from the rims of glasses and plates. Do your best to keep food and beverages sanitary and your hands clean. Make sure that the proper order gets delivered to the right guest.

IF YOU ARE NOT PROUD OF AN ORDER, DO NOT SERVE IT.

It is the responsibility of the kitchen to prepare and serve the food to very high standards. KNOW HOW EACH DISH IS TO APPEAR AND BE PRESENTED WITH GARNISH. If you are in doubt of an order, notify the chef or manager. Once you leave the kitchen with an order, it becomes your responsibility. Protect the restaurant's reputation for quality.

Make sure that the table has all the necessary silverware for the upcoming course. Also, make sure that any condiment items that the guest may need are on the table or brought to the table With the food delivery. The guest should not have to ask for these items. THIS IS VERY IMPORTANT!

Busser priorities while serving customers are as follows:

- Make coffee and iced tea.
- Fill creamers.
- Cut lemons for the coffee/tea station.
- Serve water (tap, Panna, Pellagrino) as soon as guests are seated.

- Serve bread and pate' to the table (butter or oil upon request).
- Remove plates from the table after everyone has finished with a particular course. When clearing the table, always separate the china, glassware, and flatware to avoid breakage. Dishes should be stacked according to shape and size to allow for more room on the tray or bus pan. Do not stack more than 3 or 4 plates high. Do not hold plates against your chest.
- Assist food server with refilling coffee cups, coffee pots, and water. The guest should never have to ask for more. As you are passing by other tables, look to see if other guests need refills. This makes for excellent customer service.
- Check to see (by asking customer) if more bread is needed.
- Ensure that all condiments (cream, sugar) and service supplies (lemons, teaspoons, cups, saucers) are readily available.
- Be available at all times for guests' special requests.
- Scraping crumbs from the table.
- Vacuum the carpet in your area s needed throughout your shift.
- Once the guest has departed, promptly reset the table. Tables must be reset the same way every time so that the dining room has a uniform look. Settings are to be placed as shown to you during training.
- Maintain general cleanliness of your station.

Serving Techniques

Some Standard Procedures

When possible, *serve* at the guest's right-hand side with your right hand; *remove* from the guest's left-hand side with your left hand.
Tip for remembering: **Right-Leave the food just RIGHT. Left-remove what's LEFT.**

Set up solids (bread, salad, etc.) on guest's left, and liquids (water, wine, etc.) on guest's right. Avoid reaching across and in front of a guest to serve another guest. Do not "conveniently" serve two guests (one on either side) from the same serving position. Move to the correct position for serving each guest.

When serving a large group, keep extra silver and napkins handy. Someone is going to drop something, or use all the wrong eating utensils, guaranteed.

How Is Everything?

Timing is Everything

It is appropriate to inquire once (and not every 37 seconds) shortly after the entrées are served:

"Is everything to your satisfaction, Ms. Jones?" Stop and ask sincerely, not on the run, or as and afterthought. Look your guests in the eye to assure yourself that everything is, in fact, to their satisfaction.

You're going to learn to love doing this, and because of your excellent service and critical eye, the answer will always be "Yes! Everything is perfect!" Oh happy day!

Clearing the Table

At the End of the Entrée—"May I Clear?"

When it is time to clear the main course (you should wait until everyone at the table has finished, unless a customer has deliberately pushed his/her plate aside), take everything off the table except working drinks. Salt and peppershakers, condiments and bread should never be left on the table. Clear dirty dishes putting silverware on top, so plates will stack more evenly and not slide around. **Do not stack more than 3 or 4 plates on your arm.** Dishes should not be held against your chest. Remove all empty wine glasses. When dropping off dirty dishes in the kitchen, adhere to these rules: glassware is to be placed in the appropriate racks; plates are left on the stainless steel counter along with goosenecks; and all silverware is to be placed in the tub. NO EXCEPTIONS! If there is a wine bucket on the table, take it away. Throw away the wine bottle. Place soiled napkins in the linen bag. Put empty breadbaskets next to the bread warmer.

After you have cleared the table, ask the customers if they'd care for coffee, espresso, cappuccino, dessert and/or an after dinner drink. Do not ask your busser to take any coffee and desert orders. Make sure the coffee and desserts get charged to the customer. When serving coffee or desserts, do not place the spoon or fork on the plate. Before the plate has been set down in front of the customer, place it on the correct side. If customers seem to be lingering over coffee and dessert, you might want to ask them if they would care for an after dinner drink.

The food server is responsible to replace the silverware for the up coming courses. For example: the spoon should be on the table before the food runner delivers the soup.

To Remove or Not To Remove—That is the Question

In a more formal setting, all plates per course are removed at the same time. In a more casual setting, and only after you have asked for and gotten permission, you may remove individual plates during the meal. For a couple, however, remove plates at the same time.

Use your good judgment.

Stacking

Try to avoid stacking when removing plates, especially with the slippery silverware left in between. Keep an eye on your busser in this regard.

If you can manage it, use a tray to carry everything to or away from the table in one trip. If you can't manage it, get help or make another trip.

Presenting the Check

At the End of the Meal

At lunch, when most (but not all) customers are in a hurry, present the check while they're having their coffee and/or dessert. At dinner, say nothing when presenting the check, and do not present it until the guest has either asked for it, or has declined the coffee and dessert. Do NOT ask the busser to present the check. Bussers are not permitted to handle cash or process charges.

I don't know how many times I have been presented with a check when I was looking forward to coffee and dessert. In such cases, when the guest has to ask (for dessert and/or coffee), the waiter takes the check back, of course, but the "damage" is done. The guest is left feeling rushed. Not good. Phrases such as "Take your time," or "No rush," are completely out of line and should never be used. Silence is golden at this time.

Correct Change is Your Responsibility

It is your responsibility to see that each guest receives the correct change. It is also your responsibility to see that the correct change is in the appropriate denominations.

Example: Dinner is $30 and the guest gives you $40 (two twenties). How should the change be broken down?

Solution: All ones, or a five and five ones, NEVER a ten and two fives.

I once received a $10 bill back on such a guest check situation. Since I had planned to tip 20% ($6.00), I called the inappropriate change to the waiter's attention. He mumbled something about a new cashier, which I didn't need to hear, taking a *blame-someone-else* attitude and looking pitiful at best. He took my $10 bill and returned with a five and five ones. I then tipped 12% and vowed never to return.

About Gratuities

Better known as "Tips"

(**T**o **I**nsure **P**rompt **S**ervice)

Please note: Tips should NEVER determine the quality of service.

The Situation: You have a repeat guest who never tips. NEVER dish such a guest with other staff members, and always give him or her the exact same excellent service you give to your high-tipping guests. This is the sign of a true professional.

Some people just *don't*, *can't* or *won't* tip, and that has to be okay. Complaining and whining about it is not going to change it. It doesn't make such a guest a bad person, so accept it and move on in good cheer. It all balances out in the end and you'll have what you deserve at the end of you shift.

Bussers should not pick up tips from the table. Leave tip on the table for the server to pick up.

Checking Out

Before checking out, make sure all of your side work is completed. NO ONE is to leave the restaurant without permission of the manager on duty. Anyone doing so will be subject to disciplinary action. Before signing off at the end of your shift, you must have prior approval by the manager on duty.

When you are ready to check out, follow these check out procedures:

1. Separate Credit Card Tickets, Cash Checks, Guest Comps, Manager Meals, Discounted Checks, and Gift Certificates Redeemed.
2. Credit Card Checks—Staple the guest signature ticket to the back of the payment receipt. The top receipt copy will have the printed subtotal, charge tip, tax, and payment. Paperclip all of the credit card checks together.
3. Cash checks—Staple all cash checks together.
4. Guest Comps—Make sure a manager has signed each comp. Paperclip all comp checks together.
5. Manager Meals—Make sure a manager signs for his/her meal. Paperclip all manager meal checks together.
6. Discounts—If the check is an employee discount, the employee name and manager's signature must be on the check. Employee discounts ate 50% when on duty and 25% when off duty. If an employee pays with a credit card, put the check with discounts, not credit cards. Paperclip all discounts together.
7. Gift Certificates Redeemed—Staple the gift certificate to the back of the payment receipt. Paperclip all gift certificates together.
8. Duplicate/Voided Checks—If you have a duplicate check, staple the voided check to the back of the check that was paid. The check should then be grouped with the tender group (cash, credit card, etc.). If the check was just voided, paperclip all voids together.

Put your end of shift report on top of all the above and put neatly into an envelope. If there is "cash due" at the bottom of the shift report, that amount of cash must be in the envelope. Round up or down to the next dollar. For example, if the cash due amount is $100.50, the amount in the envelope should be $101.00. If the amount is $100.49, the amount in the envelope should be $100.00. On the front of the envelope write your name, total sales amount, lunch or dinner, and the amount of cash in the envelope. A manager will verify your envelope at the end of your shift.

Closing duties include:

- Making sure the hostess podium is neat and clean.
- If another hostess is relieving you, pass on any information you may have for the day.

Serving Closing Side Work:

1. Wipe clean and fill saltshakers, peppershakers, and sugar caddies.
2. Restock garridon, silverware, and plates.
3. Wipe clean check presenters.
4. Clean computer station and back kitchen station.
5. Fold napkins: 50 pre server.
6. Remove flower vases from tables—fill with water if needed.
7. Return any chairs borrowed to their place. Place chairs along the walls; do not stack them.

Busser closing duties:

- Wipe down all condiment containers, the bread warmer, the cutting boards, and bus pans.
- Restock the linen as needed.

Remove/empty dirty lien bags, combine them together, and place them outside in linen cart.

———————————

*With thanks to Daniel N. Griesgraber.

CHAPTER 5
Offering Cocktails

If your customers already have cocktails with them when they are seated, ask them if they would like to wait a few minutes before ordering. Ask them if they would like tap water or bottled water. If bottled water, ask if they would like Panna (regular water) of Pellagrino (sparkling water). If you have customers whom you believe are under the drinking age, do not suggest cocktails or wine. If you have any doubt that they are under age, CHECK IDENTIFICATION! When in doubt, CARD! You are responsible. The penalty to you and the restaurant for serving minors is severe. If, as in most cases, the party does not already have cocktails, offer a before-dinner cocktail or wine. Direct your beverage question to the table in general, not to individuals. A very important part of your job is the offering of a cocktail before the start of a meal. Take a positive approach in your salesmanship. Treat your customers you would a guest at your home.

When taking the order, stand up. Do not lean on the table, chair, or booth. Never touch the customer. Take the women's order first. Do not leave the table until you are positive that you have taken the order correctly. If there is any doubt, repeat the order. (This is an element of your organization. Consolidate your efforts). Go to the bar and obtain drinks. You are responsible for all items delivered to the table; make sure they are entered on the check.

If your party does not want cocktails, ask them if they would care to order wine. If they do, be sure to ask if they would like their wine right away or would like to wait for their main course. Make sure you check the list (a copy of which you should jot down and carry with you) before confirming the re-order. Champagne is always served in special fluted champagne glasses. All full bottles of white wine and champagne should have an ice bucket, if available.

Note: When serving champagne, it is not necessary to offer a taste. Champagne is tasted at the winery before the final bottling takes place and airtight cork prevents it from going bad.

To save time and embarrassment, always get the necessary details at the time of order.

Example: "On the rocks, sir?"; "Would you care for a glass with your beer, Mr. Jones?"

Important: Identify each person's position at the table from which you are taking the order to prevent having to ask, "Who gets the Martini?"

A Word of Caution

When serving those tall, top-heavy fancy drinks in the flute-style glasses, NEVER try to serve off the tray. Sit the tray down, or have someone (not a guest) help you. Actually, it makes it more festive if someone does help you, but if you're alone, and there is more than one drink on the tray, you're more than likely going to have that second drink end up where you don't want it while attempting to serve drink #1. Save yourself a lot of grief and think this out.

And NEVER serve from a *bare* silver tray or the words "slip-sliding away" will have new meaning for you. Always use a *flat* (no bumps) tray liner, or a *slightly* damp cloth.

I had my singularly worse incident in all my years of serving by not obeying the above rules. As I attempted to serve one of the three tall drinks on my tray, I leaned slightly forward, pitching the other two drinks into the lap of a very prominent food critic. I was *told* to get help, but being such a "smarty," I thought I could handle it. Well, I was wrong, and was sent home, lucky to still have a job.

The Whys and Wherefores of Wine

If there is a separate wine list, please do not assume the guest wants to see it. Ask, and then proceed accordingly. If the guests decline the wine list, which should still be in your hand, then a friendly and warm, "Very good, Mr. Clark. Your captain (or waiter) will be with you in a moment," is the appropriate response.

NEVER pour or serve drinks, especially wine, unless you know how. It takes time to learn the proper techniques. Avoid looking the fool, and do not be afraid to ask for help. We all started out not knowing about such things.

NEVER pour anything without first asking permission, not even water. "May I?" So simple, yet so effective.

NEVER have your busser serve alcoholic beverages from the bar.

When you bring wine to the table, show the label to the customer and make sure he/she acknowledges it. If you have the feeling that the customer has ordered incorrectly, or is confused, mention the name of the wine as you present it, i.e., "This is 97 Silver Oak Alexander Valley"

When opening the wine bottle, it should be either placed on the table or hand held (but not against the body). Try to avoid "popping" the cork. After the bottle is opened, offer a sample to the person who ordered it. Once they approve, serve the women first, starting from the taster's right. If the customer rejects the wine, bring it to the manager on duty for a decision. Once the wine has been served, return periodically to refill the glasses.

Learn Your Wine

As we mentioned earlier, learn the stemware; take the time to do your homework.

Seek the wise counsel and advice of a willing sommelier (wine steward).

At the very least, learn the difference between red, white, and blush (other than their colors of course!). It will all pay off in the long run, and in more ways than you might expect. (See *Bibliography*)

Tips On The Tipsy

NEVER serve someone who is obviously intoxicated. Use the tried-and-true: "Please forgive me, Ms. Jones . . . I cannot serve you at this time. House rules."

By all means get help from the management if required. You may be saving Ms. Jones' life, and saving your employer from a lawsuit, to boot.

Offering Coffee and Tea

(See *Offering Cocktails*)

Again, get the necessary details. "Do you take lemon with your tea, Mr. Smith?" "Cream and sugar, Mrs. Brown?" Getting it right the first time saves a trip or two.

CHAPTER 6
Special Occasions in Serving

When There Are Children

Ignore them. Never touch them, and only speak to the little darlings as necessary, no matter how tempting it may be. In this day and age, many parents are concerned about strangers and their children. So play it safe, and stick to the above.

Also, children are real scene-stealers, and this is *your* show. You're the star of this production. You have been warned.

Serving Friends and Family

The workplace is just that and not a place to visit and chat with friends and family. Give them the same wonderful service you are giving all your other guests and nothing more. They'll understand and admire you for this most professional stance, guaranteed.

P.S.—Obviously, this is the exception to the rule of "No first names." Of course brother Bill is "Bill," an good friend Frank is "Frank." And Mom is always "Mom." I knew you could adjust to this.

"Huggy-Kissy"

In consideration of your other guests, try not to be overly huggy-kissy with old friends, long-time customers, and/or family, unless, of course, it's your mother, or you're huggy-kissy with all your guests. Be equal in your attention, be it old friends or new friends. It's only fair.

Now, if they are huggy-kissy with you first, accept it graciously, and then move on.

Serving Large Parties

Check with the host or hostess of the group: Do they want "ladies first" service, or the more formal "serve to the right of the hostess" where the guest of honor, if there is one, would be seated—continuing on with the hostess being served last? If the hostess is also the guest of honor, then, and only then, would she be served first.

If there is a host *and* hostess, again the hostess is served *last*, and the host is served second to last. In other words, if not "ladies first," and there is a host and hostess, sitting at opposite ends of the table from each other, which is the correct seating for a formal sit-down dinner, then you would serve to the hostess's right until you reach the host.

At this point, stop, do not serve the host at this time, and begin again, at the hostess's left, and serve until you once more reach the host. Now you may serve the host. Finally, return and serve the hostess.

If the host is also the guest of honor, serve him first, wherever he is sitting.

Practice this procedure mentally at an empty table for 10 or so, visualizing the hostess at the head of the table and the host at the foot of the table, facing each other. You'll get the idea. However, if somewhere along the line, the host of hostess blurts out "Where's mine?" go immediately to Plan B, and without further ado or comment, serve them as quickly as possible with a standard, "Please forgive me"—unflustered and with a smile.

If the host and hostess are sitting side by side, the above still applies; i.e., serve to their right until you arrive back to them; *then* serve the host (second to last), and then the hostess, who is last.

If there is both a host and hostess, always defer to the hostess, unless directed otherwise, or it will be very obvious the host is running the show. Always adjust accordingly. These days, the host usually handles the bill, etc.. However, deferring to the hostess is the more formal procedure. You may never get to experience this formal service. Too bad, it was all very grand; but at least mow you have the knowledge of how it was.

The Lonely-Heart

Be on the alert of Mr. or Ms. Lonely-heart, sitting solo and probably feeling a little sorry for themselves. Be kind, be gentle, be loving, and be brief. Remember, they may ask, but they really don't want to hear about you. They really want *you* to hear about *them*. So be patient, and as attentive as time will allow, keeping in mind that someday you may be the one sitting alone in that chair.

You might want to use any influence you have to assure that those Lonely-hearts don't get stuck with that awful table halfway into the kitchen, just past the service stand. You can save that one for the couple in the shorts, wearing shower clogs, and matching plastic fanny packs. You know the ones.

A NOTE TO ALL CONCERNED (Management, Maitre d', Host/Hostess, Captain, Waiters, and Bussers) RE: THE LONE DINER . . .

It is very rude, insulting, and inappropriate to use the term, "*Just* one?" The correct and only appropriate term is "*Party of one*, Mr. Knight?" You would not say "*Just* a party of 15?" would you?

CHAPTER 7
Work Well With Others

Take Care When Dealing with Others

Be aware of ethnic and religious differences, preferences, and customs, and not just regarding food. Pointing your finger at a member of your dinner party, for example, would be considered taboo in many cultures. And addressing a woman directly, instead of going through her husband, can be offensive to others. You'll learn, as you go along, and, as always, don't be afraid to ask.

Dealing With the Boss

Don't argue with your manager, you aren't going to win; nor should you. That's why your manager is called "the boss." The best route to the boss's *heart*, and every boss does have one, is through a sincere approach for help. In other words, ask your manager to help you with *whatever* the problem is, even if it is one involving "the boss."

If you have a manager or supervisor who constantly berates you, raises his or her voice at you, scolds you, corrects you, or in any way humiliates you in front of guests or fellow staff members, you may want to start looking for a position elsewhere. Your days are probably numbered anyway.

Unless it is a real emergency, never accept a personal call at work. Handle any personal calls on break, or at the end of the shift. And use a pay phone, or your own cell phone, please.

Chapter 8
Unusual Situations

Even if you follow all of the instructions in this manual, unusual situations may occasionally arise. The following are a list of the more common situations you may encounter and how to deal with them.

REMEMBER: Rule #1. Never argue with a customer! Get the manager, explain the situation, and let him/her work things out if you have a problem.

- Food Sent Back
  If a customer sends back an item other than for reheating, get the manager to check the item first, and then have the manager go with you to the kitchen to have things straightened out. Do not throw the item away until the chef has seen it.
- Complaints About Food (but not sent back)
- If a customer complains about something but does not want to send it back, notify the manager. Some adjustments will be made.
- Wine Sent Back
  Notify the manager.
- Drinks Sent Back
  Bring the drink back to the bartender and explain the situation. Notify the manager if this becomes a regular occurrence.
- Mistaken Orders
  If a customer claims he/she ordered something other than what you brought, do not argue—get what he/she wants! (If the order was taken carefully and you repeated the order where you are going. Excessive breakage through carelessness is grounds for disciplinary action.

Accidents/Spilling/Etc.

If you drop of spill something on a customer, or accidentally knock someone over (it happens), your first consideration should be the customer's well being. If you spill something, get a damp cloth and let the customer wipe them self off. Never touch the customer, unless it is to remove something that has fallen. Notify the manager as soon as possible. He/she will make any adjustments regarding cleaning costs, insurance, etc.. Avoid discussing who was at fault. Above all, tend to matters quietly and discreetly with as little commotion or disturbance as possible.

Chapter 9
General Information, Rules, and Policies*

Below is a suggested outline of company policies and procedures that would apply to all employees. You would also receive additional information specific to your job classification. These are all excellent examples.

Time Clock

1. All hourly employees must be clocked in when they are working. In order to be paid for the correct number of hours every week, you must clock in and clock out in the MICROS system each day you work. *This is you responsibility.* Failure to clock in or out will result in disciplinary action.
2. Employees can clock in no more than 10 minutes prior to their scheduled start time.
3. All early-outs for employees must have a Manager's approval. *No Exceptions!*

Employee Meals & Breaks

1. Employees will receive a 50% discount on their meals while on duty. You will also receive a 25% discount when you (and up to three guests) dine in the restaurant while off duty.
2. At times management may prepare special meals, which will be provided to the employees at no charge.

3. Employee meals are to be consumed in Back of the House areas only, usually in the area that is not visible to the guest, unless the Restaurant is closed to the public. Exceptions will be made if all the non-visible space is in use. Employees are expected to clean up after themselves.

4. Employees will receive a paid 15—minute break after four hours of word. If an employee is scheduled to work 8 or more hours, they will receive a 30 minute lunch break (not paid). The employee must clock out for their lunch break.

Punctuality & Attendance

If an employee is unable to work, he/she must advise a *manager* at least two (2) hours prior to the start of the shift to allow the manager time to make adjustments for the absence.

Excessive absenteeism will be dealt with in a fair and consistent manner. When an employee's attendance record exceeds 6 absences in a 12 month period and/or displays a pattern of absenteeism, it will be considered "excessive absenteeism." The 12-month period starts from time of first absence. Each incident will stay on an employee's record for one year.

If the employee's absence continues for more than one day, it is his/her responsibility to call each day so that the supervisor has a clear understanding about the probable date of return. A letter from a doctor will be required if the employee is absent for medical reasons for 3 consecutive days, or if the employee shows a pattern of excessive absenteeism.

The policy for attendance and punctuality will be enforced as follows:

Third incident	Written coaching
Fourth incident	Written warning
Fifth incident	Final written warning
Sixth incident	Three-day suspension
Seventh incident	Separation from employment

An attendance and punctuality calendar for each staff member will be maintained. Punctuality will be handled on the same fair and consistent manner as attendance, but will be separate when considering corrective action. Excessive tardiness is a separate offense and will be handled suing appropriate action.

A "No Call No show" is considered a voluntary separation from employment. An employee may be reinstated with a verifiable, reasonable excuse as to why they could not adhere to the call procedure.]

Appearance

It is essential that all employees be well groomed in order to present a neat, clean, and professional appearance to customers. Hair must be clean, neat, and groomed. Extreme hairstyles are not allowed. For males, your face must be clean-shaven, unless you wear a beard, in which case it must be kept trimmed. Your overall appearance must be neat, clean, and fresh. If an employee is dressed inappropriately, he/she will be sent home to change into suitable attire. A smile is part is your uniform and is required whenever serving the public.

*Special note on appearance and demeanor: Please, do not play with your hair, keep your hands out of your pockets, and dress appropriately and professionally. Leave expensive jewelry at home. For the ladies—do not wear tight clothes and watch that cleavage. Remember, you're working, not looking for a date!

Uniforms:

1. Uniforms must be neat, clean, and in good repair, free of wrinkles.
2. Slacks are required for Front of the House employees.
3. Shoes are to be black, non-skid type. Stockings or socks are to be worn at all times—free of runs, holes, etc..
4. Jewelry and make-up is to be conservative. While on duty, you cannot wear earrings of any kind anywhere except in the earlobes. This includes the nose, mouth, cheek, eyes, belly button, tongue, and any other part of your body that is visible to customers. No excessive dangles. Males may wear non-dangle type earrings only.
5. Non-uniform personnel are to dress in a business-like fashion.

6. Tattoos must be covered. (Arms, neck, hand, legs, and any other place on the body that the guest can see.)
7. Uniforms are provided for most classifications. It is the employees' responsibility to clean and maintain their uniforms. The uniforms must be returned upon separation with the company prior to your receiving your final paycheck. There will be a $150 charge for each uniform not returned in usable condition.

Behavior

1. Courtesy is a must at all times.
2. Do not socialize with co-workers, friends, or customers while on duty, unless it is directly related to your job.
3. Using, possessing, or selling alcoholic beverages or illegal drugs during work hours are prohibited.
4. Subscribe to a drug-free work environment. All employees are subject to reasonable cause drug testing.
5. Smoking is prohibited while on duty unless on lunch or breaks. Smoking while on lunch or breaks is allowed outside only.
6. Theft, in any instance, will be cause for immediate termination.
7. Violating any rules/policies or not complying with your Job Description, at the judgment and discretion of management, will result in the issuance of a Coaching Document. Upon a second offense, there will be a written warning. Upon a third offense, there will be a final warning with a suspension. If there is a fourth offense, it is cause for immediate termination.
8. Employees are not allowed to make personal calls while on duty unless approved by a manager. This includes the use of company phones and personal cell phones. You are allowed to use your cell phone while on break, however cell phones are to be locked up while punched in.

Safety

Safety is everyone's responsibility. The management staff is committed to providing a safe working environment for all of our employees. Employees are expected to obey safety rules, follow safe work practices, and exercise caution in all their work activities. If you see a spill, wipe it up to avoid a slip hazard for you your co—workers. Report any unsafe condition to your manager immediately.

Cash Variances

Any cash discrepancy, whether it is overage or shortage, needs to be brought to the attention of your manager immediately.

1. Shortage(s) over $10 in one day or $25 in two weeks will result in a verbal warning.
2. The second offense will result in a written warning with restitution.
3. The third offense will result in a final written warning with restitution.
4. The fourth offense will result in separation from employment with restitution.
5. A shortage of $50 or more in one day will result in suspension, pending investigation and/or could result in termination of employment with restitution.

Vacation/Days Off

The following procedures for vacations and days off requests will give all of the staff the opportunity to plan in advance for their personal needs.

1. Any day off request must be turned in 7 days in advance of the week you are requesting time off.
2. All vacations must be submitted 14 days in advance of the week you are requesting vacation.
3. If you call in sick on a day you requested off, but was denied, you must provide a doctor's slip or some type of documentation that helps confirm this was an unavoidable absence. Attendance policy will still apply.

We will approve or disapprove the vacation request within 5 days from the receipt of your request. It is your responsibility to check with your manager to make sure it was approved.

We will always take requests for emergency time off under consideration at any time.

Schedules/Payday

1. Management assigns schedules in the interest of providing excellent customer service while maintaining prudent cost control. Schedules are posted on Fridays prior to next week starting. Days off can be altered at the discretion of management. No days off are permanent or guaranteed. It is your responsibility to check your schedule and be at your assigned station on time. Your manager must approve any schedule changes.
2. There will be staff meetings periodically as announced by management.

Unauthorized Discounts

1. Except when expressly authorized by the General Manager, it is forbidden to give any person or cause any person to receive Company property, including but not limited to food or beverage, without proper charge or payment.
2. It is likewise forbidden to accept aforementioned company property or products without proper charge or payment.
3. Disciplinary action for this offense will be of a severe nature and handled on a case-by-case basis.
4. The only exception to this rule are that employees are permitted to consume coffee, tea, or soda in non-public areas.

General Information

1. It is the responsibility of each employee to provide his/her own supplies that are required to do their job (writing utensils, crumber, corkscrew, etc.).
2. Random checks will be made by management.
3. All employees are required to cooperate and assist co-workers if the need arises. Teamwork is essential to a successful operation. In case of any problem, discuss it in private with your manager.
4. Communication is very important in any organization. If you have a question, problem, concern, or suggestion, discuss it with your manager. If you do not get an answer from your manager, or wish

to pursue a higher authority, you may discuss your issue with the general manager.

5. General and specific information will be posted on your department bulletin board. It is you responsibility to check the board daily for new postings.

6. Non-bar employees are not permitted behind the bar at any time, except when authorized by management.

7. Intentionally damaging, breaking, or abusing company property will result in termination. Excessive accidental damages will result in disciplinary action.

8. Lost & Found items should be turned in to the manager. A cabinet is in the general manager's office for these items.

A breach or violation of certain rules may also constitute a crime. An arrest or conviction for a criminal offense is not necessary to validate or justify discipline, including discharge, for a violation of employee rules.

When a question is raised regarding the meaning or application of any employment rule or any other policy or procedure, management may discuss it with the employee, but management retains the right to make the final determination as to the meaning or application of the rule.

The foregoing rules are illustrative and not exhaustive. Management has the right to determine whether particular conduct, which may not be described on these rules, is not in the best interest of the company or its operations and therefore warrants disciplinary action or separation from employment. Management has the sole right to determine the type of discipline, if any. In addition, whether the particular conduct contradicts any of these rules or not will be determined solely by management.

Thank you and welcome to the team

After reading the above rules and policies, employee must sign the attached signature sheet and return to the Administration Office. By signing you are acknowledging that you have received this manual, understand its contents, and will adhere to the rules and policies it contains.

General information, Rules, & Policies Signature Sheet

(To be removed from the manual, signed by employee, and turned in to the Administration office to be kept in the employee's personnel file.)

I have received copy of Rules & Policies and understand its contents.

Employee Name _____

Employee Signature _____ Date _____

Hiring Manager_____ Date _____

*With thanks to Nick Tomasello.

CHAPTER 10
Moving On

You have just given, for whatever reason, your two-weeks notice (and *always* give a two-weeks notice).

You now have three choices:

1. Continue on just doing your job for the next two weeks.
2. Be a total jerk and goof off for the next two weeks.
3. Really shine and do an outstanding job in the final two weeks.

Which of these three choices will make you feel good about yourself, leave your superior wishing you weren't leaving, and set up the best possible references? Your choice should be easy, but you would be surprised how many people foolishly choose number 1 or 2.

Which would you rather have said about you, as a reference: "He was an outstanding employee." Or "I'm sorry, I could not recommend him for rehire."

It's up to you . . . it's YOUR future.

CHAPTER 11
Final notes and Comments

NEVER, ever, argue with your guests. Excuse yourself if and when you feel an argument coming on; walk calmly and with composure toward your manager, and apprise him or her of the situation.

Never raise your voice or give any indication that all is not well. And don't wait until the situation gets out of hand; let your manager nip it in the bud.

Should you ignore the above and find you're in over your head, you let yourself get too emotional or out of control, you really *must* get management involved. After all, that's what they're paid for.

Always ignore any sexual comments, innuendos, propositions, or advances. If guest persists, go to management. This is sexual harassment; you don't have to put up with it, and it's against the law.

EPILOGUE

There are always exceptions to the rules; let common sense prevail.

Easy does it and let it flow from your heart. Let it go if you're hurt, angry, or upset. Go lovingly through your shift and you will shine like the star you are. Have fun, be kind, and enjoy what you do, as you do it. Give it your best and you'll be just fine.

Remember, not everyone is cut out to be a professional waiter. Most people don't have the talent for it.

If you find that being a waiter is not for you, get out and go back to school. Get into something steady, like real estate or acting.

Appendix I

Sexual Harassment Overview and Employee Rights

Sexual Harassment occurs when one employee makes continued, unwelcome sexual advances, requests for sexual favors, and other verbal or physical conduct of a sexual nature, to another employee, against his or her wishes. According to the U.S. Equal Employment Opportunity Commission (EEOC), Sexual Harassment occurs "when submission to or rejection of this conduct explicitly or implicitly affects an individual's employment, unreasonably interferes with an individual's work performance, or creates an intimidating, hostile, or offensive work environment,"

Sexual Harassment refers to a variety of workplace offenses.

- An employee harassing another employee can be an individual of the same sex. Sexual Harassment is a gender-neutral violation.
- The harasser can be the employee's supervisor, manager, customer, co-worker, supplier, peer, or vendor.
- The direct recipient of harassment is not the only employee who is affected. An employee who observes or learns about harassment in the workplace may file a Sexual Harassment complaint.

If you experience these or related forms of Sexual Harassment as an employee, you have the following rights.

- Tell the person or persons who are responsible for the harassment to stop doing so.
- If the harassment does not stop. Immediately bring the matter to the attention of your manager.

- If the harassment comes form a manager, immediately bring the matter to the attention of one of the managing members.

What You Can Expect From Your Employer

- Immediate investigation of the allegation.
- Protection from potential retaliation, whether it is from the person accused of harassment or any other employee.
- Protection of the rights of those employees who report they are being harassed and the rights of those being accused of harassment.
- Investigations handled discreetly, confidentially, and thoroughly.
- Appropriate corrective action according to findings.
- Documentation of each case retained in permanent files.

If you have subjected to sexual harassment or any other intimidating or hostile act while working, notify your manager immediately.

A breach or violation of certain rules may also constitute a crime. An arrest or conviction for a criminal offense is not necessary to validate or justify discipline, including discharge, for a violation of employee rules.

When a question is raised regarding the meaning or application of any employment rule or any other policy or procedure, management may discuss it with the employee, but management retains the right to make the final determination as to the meaning or application of the rule.

The foregoing rules are illustrative and not exhaustive. Management has the right to determine whether particular conduct, which may not be described in these rules, is not in the best interest of the company or its operations and therefore warrants disciplinary action or separation from employment. Management has the sole right to determine the type of discipline, if any. In addition, whether the particular conduct contradicts any of these rules or not will be determined solely be management.

After reading the above rules and policies, employee must sign the attached signature sheet and return to the Administration Office. By signing you are acknowledging that you have received this sexual harassment material, understand its contents, and will adhere to the rules and policies it contains.

Sexual Harassment Signature Sheet

(To be removed from the manual, signed by employee, and turned in to the Administration office to be kept in the employee's personnel file.)

I have received copy of Sexual Harassment Overview and Employee Rights and understand its contents.

Employee Name _____

Employee Signature _____ Date _____

Hiring Manager _____ Date _____

Appendix II

Saving a Life

There may be times you'll be called upon, or simply take it upon yourself, to go above and beyond the call of duty. At such times, you, and your guest or co-worker, will be glad you know CPR, insufflation (rescue breathing), or the Heimlich maneuver.

When Someone Needs Help Immediately

Insufflation (Rescue Breathing)

1. Always check if air passage is blocked. If so, clear immediately by striking victim sharply on back, between shoulder blades; or dislodge the obstruction, which may be something he ate, or his tongue, with your fingers. While you are doing this:
2. Send someone to call 911 and check if there's a doctor in the house.
3. Check for consciousness. Tap victim and shout to see of victim responds.
4. Look, listen, and feel for breathing for about 5 seconds.
5. If victim is not breathing, or you can't tell, position victim on floor on back, while supporting head and neck with one hand.
6. Tilt victim's head back and lift chin so that the lower teeth are higher than the upper teeth. This will help open victim's airway. A folded-up coat or jacket, placed beneath the victim's *shoulders*, will help maintain this position. Again, look, listen, and feel for any signs of breathing now that the airway is open.

7. If still not breathing, place your mouth completely over victim's mouth and give 2 slow breaths.
8. Check for pulse (5-8 seconds), and repeat rescue breath.
9. If still no breath, recheck position of victim's head (#6 above) and repeat numbers 7 and8 until professional help arrives.

CPR: Cardiopulmonary Resuscitation (Heart and Breathing Rescue Technique)

1. Make sure victim is unconscious by tapping his chest, shouting, gently shaking his shoulders.
2. Tell someone to call 911 and check if there's a doctor in the house. Note: Be sure the actual address of the restaurant, and the phone number, is clearly posted on every phone for ease in giving that information when calling for help.
3. Position the victim for CPR, flat on his/her back, on floor.
4. Open the airway by placing one palm on victim's forehead, and lifting chin with other hand until teeth are almost together, but mouth is left slightly open. This may be all that's needed for the person to resume breathing. Note: If there is a neck injury, do not tilt head back; move the tongue out of the airway with your fingers.
5. Check for breathing. Look, listen, and feel; place your cheek next to victim's mouth and nose. If no sign of breathing after several seconds, repeat #4 above, checking for any obstruction, such as a piece of food, a slipped denture, etc..
6. Mouth-to-mouth: Pinch victim's nostrils together; take a deep breath, and place your open mouth completely over victim's mouth. Exhale forcefully into victim's mouth. Repeat 4 times.
7. Check for pulse at side of neck, between Adam's apple and neck muscle, for about 5 to 10 seconds. If no pulse . . .
8. Begin chest compressions: Kneel to victim, midway between shoulder and waist. Place your "weaker" hand on chest, palm pads over tip of the breastbone, with stronger hand on top, for better compressions. Lock elbows and bear down, pushing in 1.5 to 2 inches, and releasing, 5 times, to the count of 1 and 2 and 3 and 4 and 5. You should complete five compressions in about five seconds.
9. Do 15 compressions in a row, counting to 5, three times.

10. Reposition the head as in #4 above, pinch the nostrils, and again give two strong breaths, mouth-to-mouth.
11. Resume the position for chest compressions; give 15 more.
12. After 4 cycles of compressions and breathing (one set each of breathing and compressions equal one cycle), check for pulse and breathing. If neither has returned, resume the CPR. If help does not arrive promptly, see if someone else can take over for a short while.

Baby Modifications

1. Use table, or your lap, instead of floor.
2. Do everything much more gently. Necks are fragile; breaths should be puffs.
3. Place your mouth over baby's nose *and* mouth together. After each puff, be sure chest is rising. If not, airway needs to be cleared with modified Heimlich maneuver or modified blow between shoulder blades.
4. Check for pulse in baby's armpit, inside of the upper arm.
5. If a pulse, but no breathing, continue puffs at the rate of one every three seconds.
6. If no pulse, you must add compressions. Position the middle three fingers of your free hand (other is supporting baby's head) in the middle of the chest, just below nipples (feel for breastbone). Compress chest .5 to 1 inch, depending on the size of baby, almost twice as fast as on adults. Do 5 compressions (in about 3 seconds) to every 1 breath: 1 and 2 and 3 and 4 and 5 and puff.

Universal Signals of Distress

- Clutching at throat
- Being unable to speak
- Turning blue in a matter of minutes
- Losing consciousness

The Heimlich Maneuver

(First Aid for Choking, Adult/Child over 1)

1. Ask victim if he can talk or cough. If yes, he may want to clear throat without your help. However, stand by in case the situation worsens.
2. If victim cannot answer, this is a life-threatening situation. Someone should dial 911 and check to see if there is a doctor in the house while you advise victim you are going to help, with his permission.
3. Never poke at anything lodged in victim's throat. You may end up making matters worse by forcing the object deeper into the throat.
4. Have victim stand, and position yourself behind him. Grab victim around waist, just under the rib cage. Make a fist with one hand, thumb and fingers facing abdomen, and grasp fist hand at wrist with other hand.
5. Keeping elbows out, press fist with a quick thrusting motion, inward and upward. This thrust is intended to clear the victim's airway by forcing air up and out the windpipe, dislodging the obstruction.
6. Repeat Maneuver until throat is clear. If the victim loses consciousness, you can continue by kneeling over the face-up victim, with a modified thrust, or turning the victim to side and striking sharply between shoulder blades. If obstruction is dislodged, but the victim has no pulse, start CPR.

"GET THEE TO A LIBRARIEE"
Bibliography

Beverage and food services. Culinary Institute of America.

Gold, C. & Wolfman, P. (2000). *The perfect setting.* New York: Harry N Abrams.

Post, E. L. & wink, L. (2000). *The wine guide.* Time-Life Books.

Wine Service. Culinary Institute of America.

Zraly, K. (2006). *Windows on the world complete wine course.* Sterling.

Online

Have a question or two on wine?

E-mail F. Paul Pacult at *PACULT@INTERPORT.NET*

Or write Mr. Pacult at
GOOD LIBATIONS
1301 Carolina St.
Greensboro, North Carolina 27401

He's the expert and he invites your questions.

DISCLAIMER

The term "waiter" as used herein refers to all waitpersons and is meant to be all-inclusive.

ABOUT THE AUTHOR

Larry knight has recently retired as Senior Butler, Bellagio Hotel, Las Vegas, NV.

He has done it all—progressing from busboy to dishwasher to waiter to maitre d' to management to owner to Butler-to-the-Stars.

He now offers the fruits of his 50 years' experience and his many observations along the way. For God's sake, take advantage of it!

Ask about our "Train the Trainer" program.

For a live presentation and in-depth review on this material, please contact:

"On the Town, Inc."
310 Market Street #1402
San Diego, CA 92101

E-mail: *larryknight825@msn.com*

Let us bring it to life for you and your staff.

(See *Bibliography*)

Acknowledgment

Daniel Griesgraber

Nick Tomasello
For their input and contributions.

Appeal Media
Tracy Ochoa, Caserae Ochoa, and Mika Ortega
For all their support and hard work.

Steve & Tina Gibson
For their support and belief in this project.

To all: A heart felt "Thank you!"

46510074R00044

Made in the USA
Middletown, DE
02 August 2017